ALPHABET ZENTANGLES

Mindfulness & Alphabet Colouring Book

BLACKLINE MASTERS

Junior Primary

This Book Belongs to...

© Centre for Mindful Education Pty Ltd
www.centreformindfuleducation.com
All rights reserved.
No copies or distribution via print or
electronic means is permitted.

COPYRIGHT PERMSISSIONS

This book is a Blackline Master and may be photocopied or printed for personal, classroom, or distance learning use.

No parts of this book can be distributed for any other purposes through print or electronic means.

© Centre for Mindful Education Pty Ltd
www.centreformindfuleducation.com
All rights reserved.

The Secrets of Mindful Colouring

Did you know there are many benefits to mindful colouring?

The process of colouring (particularly with patterns and abstract designs) requires attention to what you are doing right now. It gives our mind something to focus on besides our busy thoughts and worries.

When we are focussed and enjoying something, we relax and feel calmer. Time seems to disappear, and the only thing we are focussed on is what we are presently doing.

This is being 'In the Zone'.

Mindful or Mind-FULL colouring?

Mindful colouring means paying attention to the action of colouring, the way the pencil moves, the way the colours blend, the movement of your hand.

If our attention is on the colouring, we are being mindful.

If our attention is on our thoughts, we are being mind-FULL.

How to colour mindfully.

Pay attention to what you are doing. Choose a colour carefully that you think will look nice on the page. Watch the way the pencil moves as you colour. See how the colour appears on the paper. Be careful to stay within the lines.
What colours look nice together?
How does your page make you feel?

We hope your students enjoy learning the alphabet while they mindfully colour

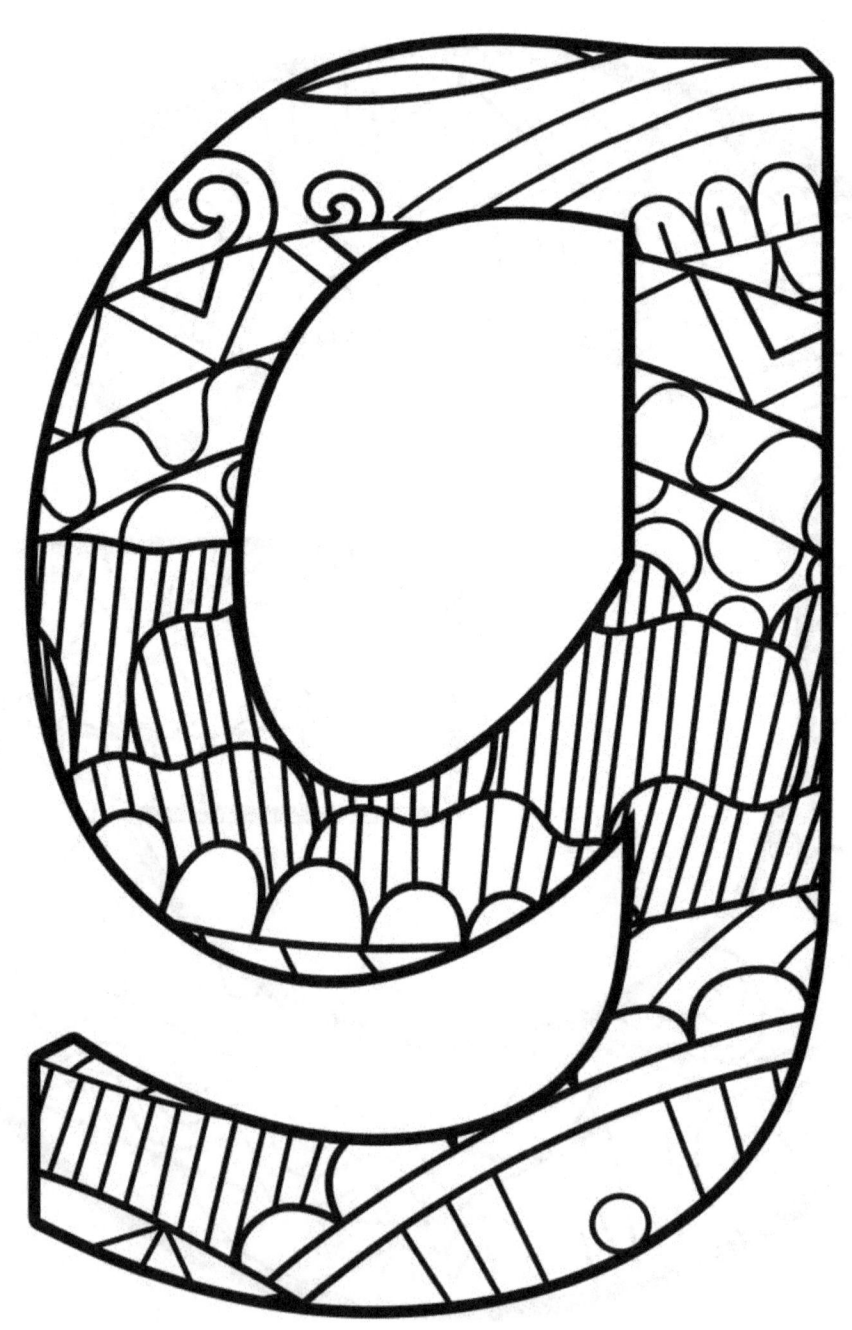

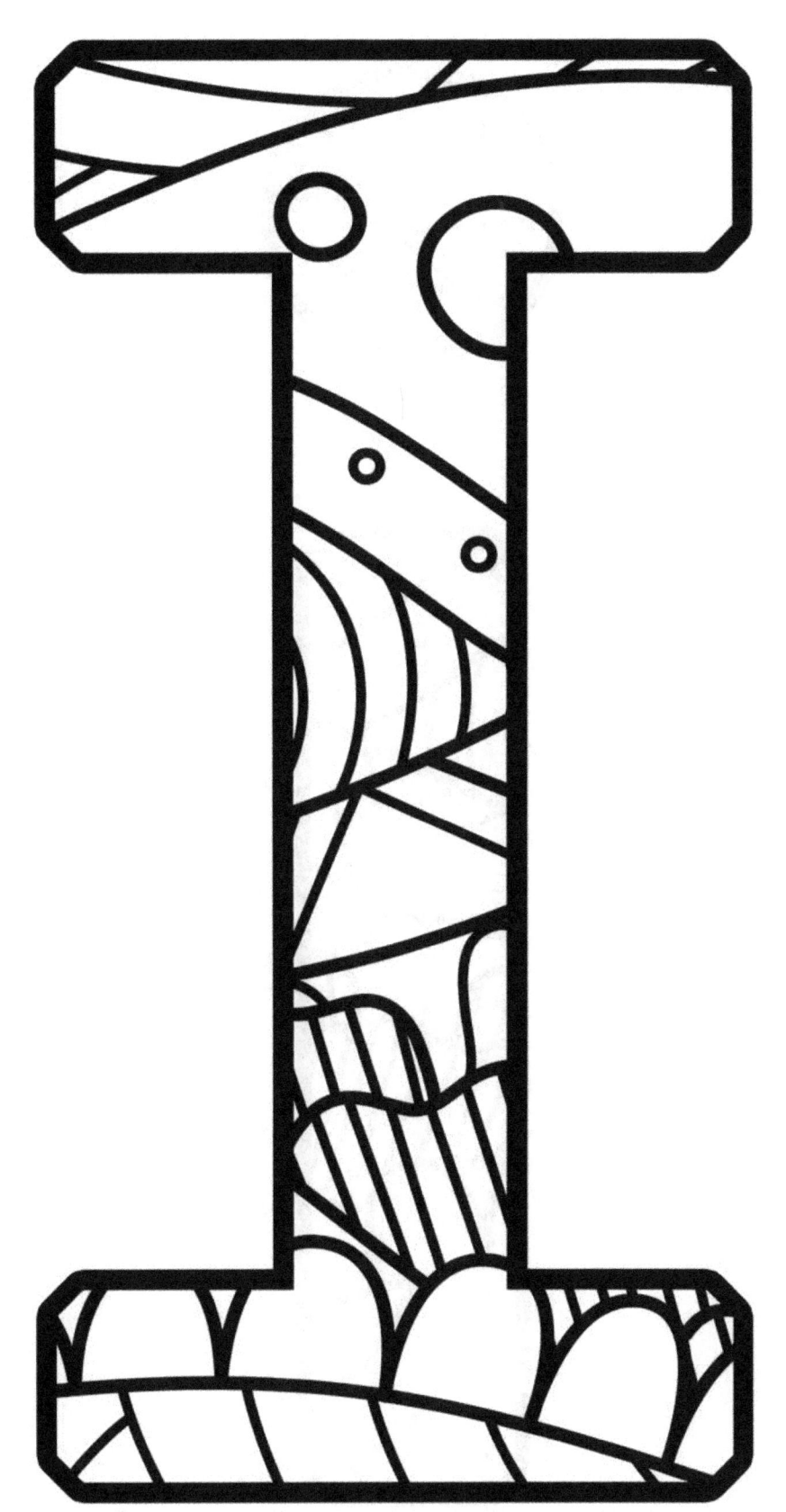

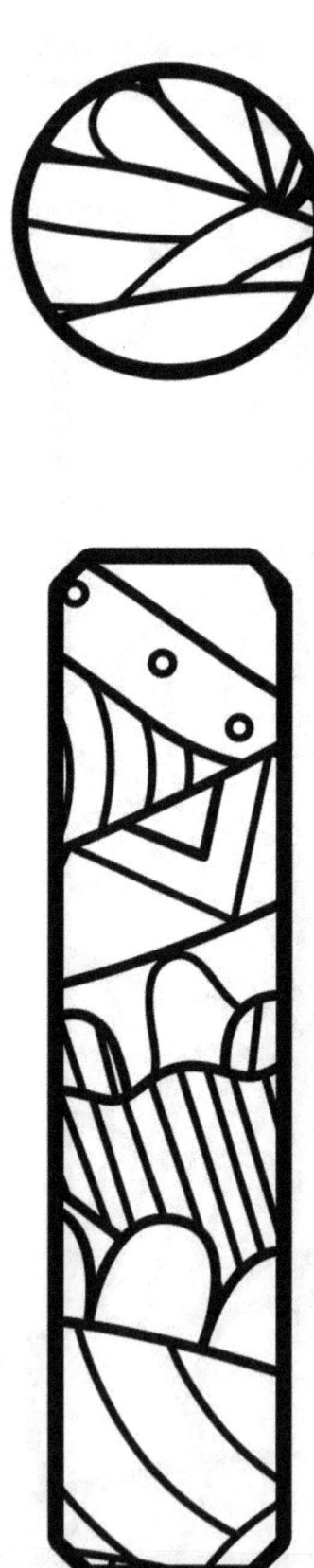

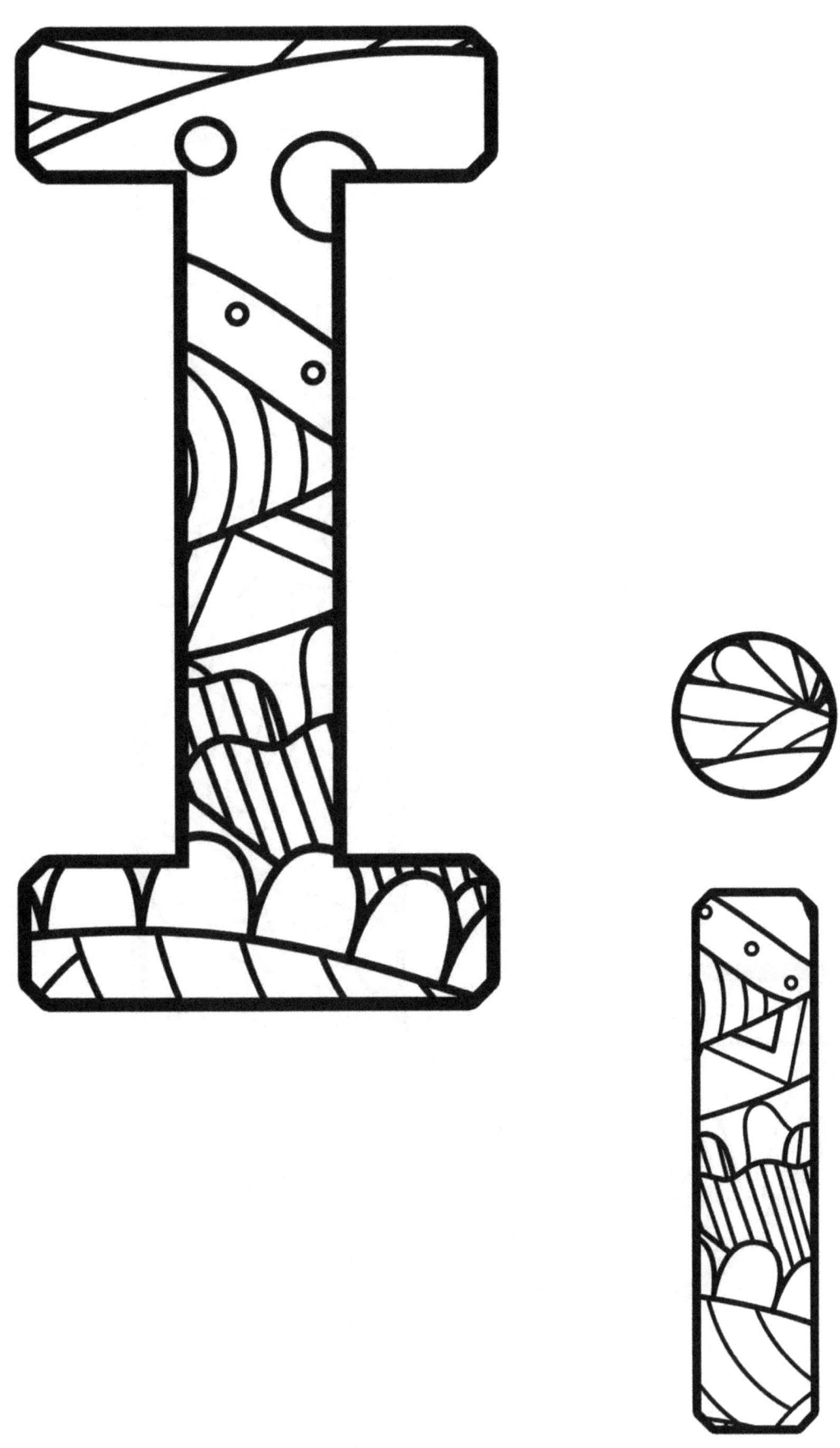

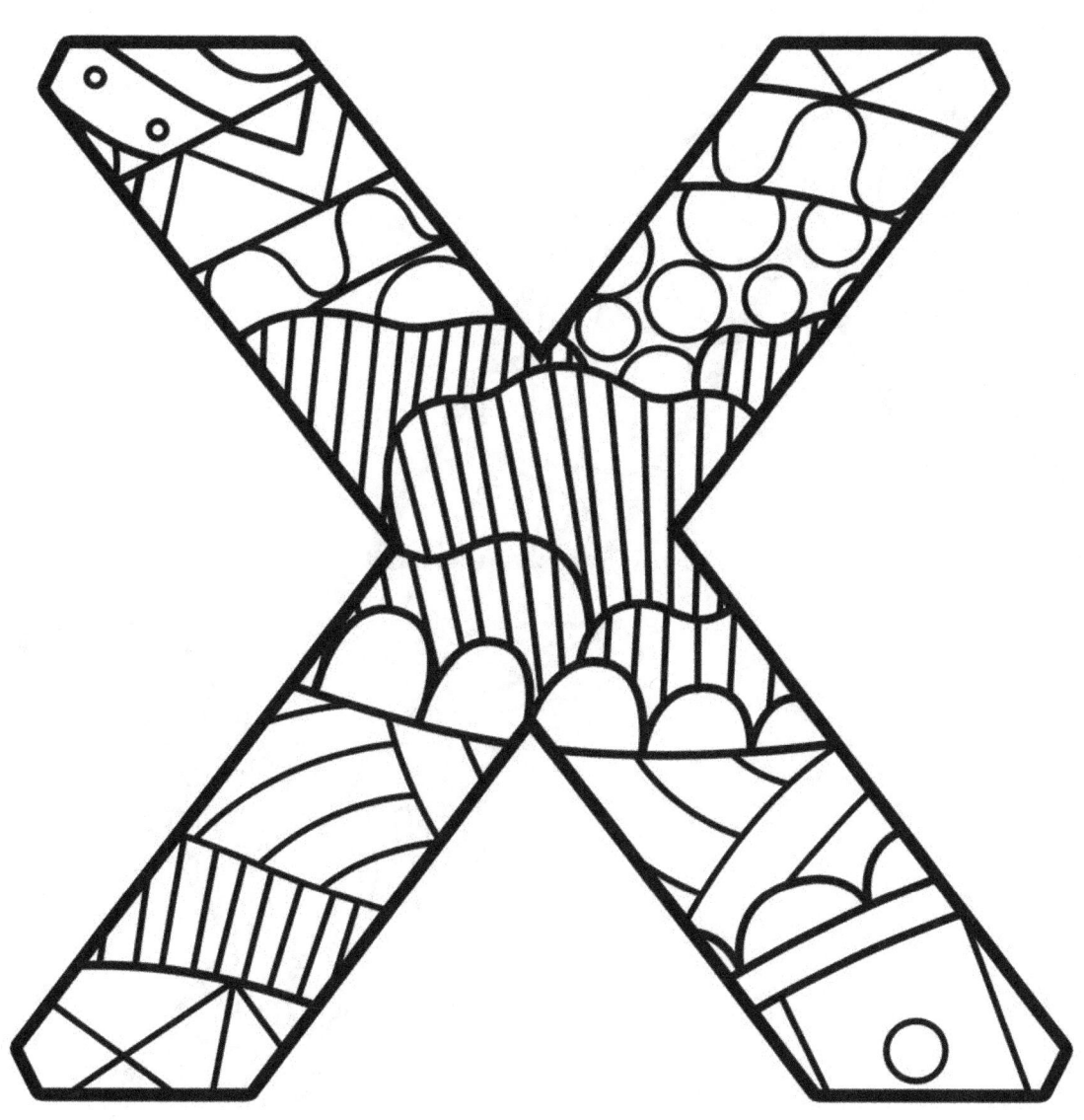

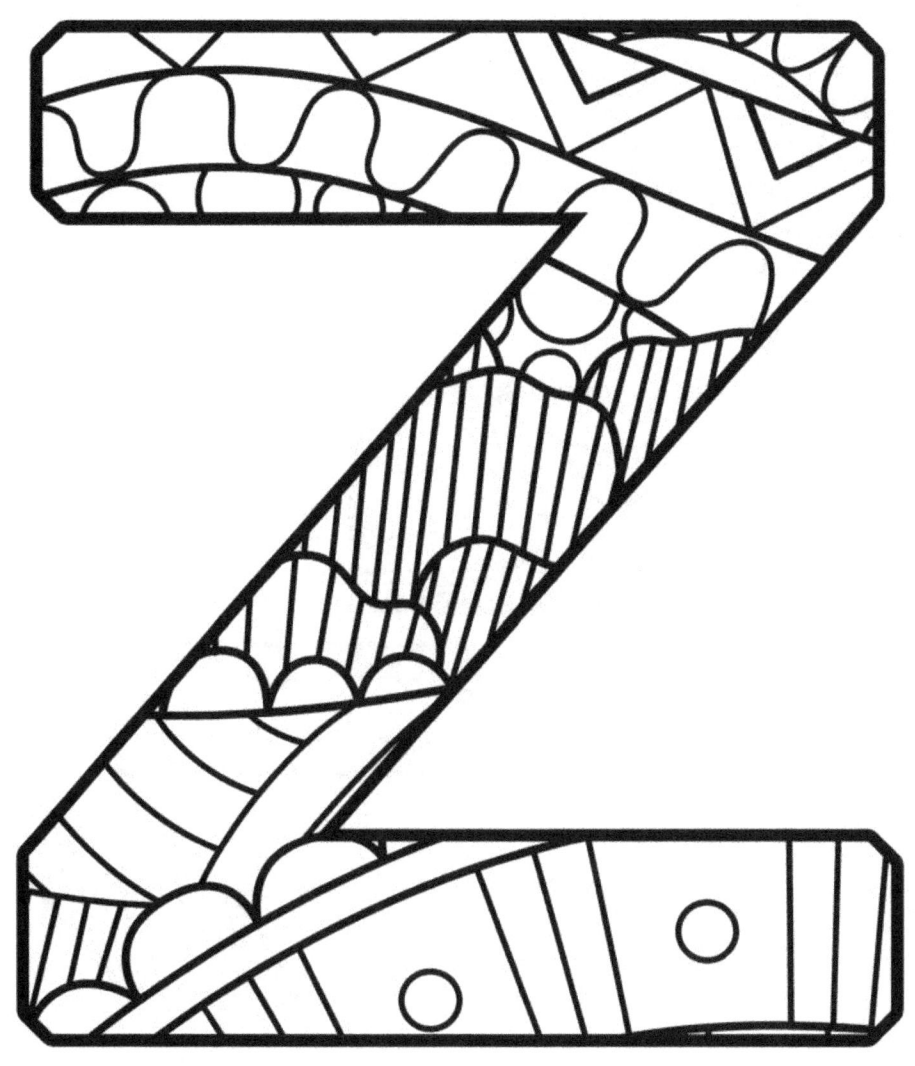

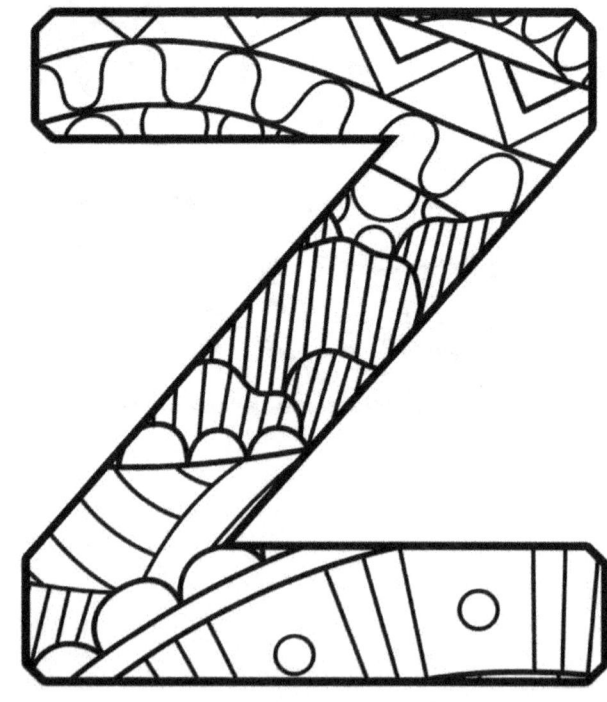

Other Titles from Centre for Mindful Education

We hope that you have enjoyed this book.

About Us
The Centre for Mindful Education is an Australian-based company with a vision is to inspire, support and guide educators who are seeking to nurture a mindfulness journey, for themselves, and for the children and students in their care.

'Our Class Gratitude Journal' Series for the Classroom

Junior Primary　　　　　　　　　Middle Primary　　　　　　　　　Upper Primary

'In the Zone' Mindfulness Colouring Books for Kids

Beginner　　　　　　　　　Intermediate　　　　　　　　　Advanced

To find out more about us please visit our website is www.centreformindfuleducation.com

To receive updates on new titles please email us at centreformindfuleducation@gmail.com

www.ingramcontent.com/pod-product-compliance
Lightning Source LLC
LaVergne TN
LVHW061346060426
835512LV00012B/2587